Beyond the Players
Coaches

by Allan Morey

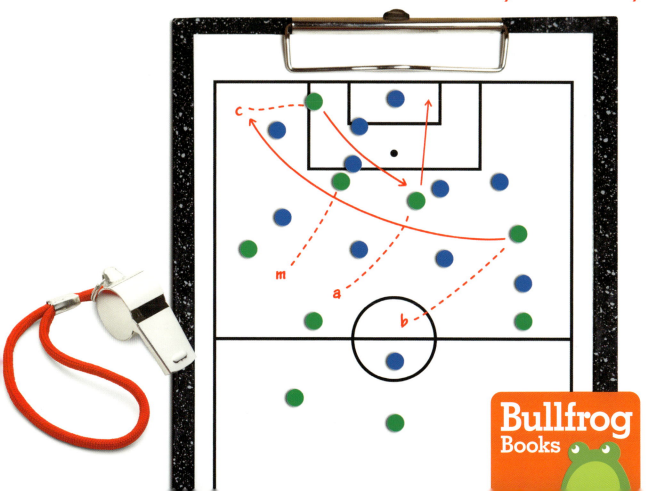

Ideas for Parents and Teachers

Bullfrog Books let children practice reading informational text at the earliest reading levels. Repetition, familiar words, and photo labels support early readers.

Before Reading
- Discuss the cover photo. What does it tell them?
- Look at the picture glossary together. Read and discuss the words.

Read the Book
- "Walk" through the book and look at the photos. Let the child ask questions. Point out the photo labels.
- Read the book to the child, or have him or her read independently.

After Reading
- Prompt the child to think more. Ask: Have you seen a coach at a live game or on TV? How do you think coaches help players?

Bullfrog Books are published by Jump!
5357 Penn Avenue South
Minneapolis, MN 55419
www.jumplibrary.com

Copyright © 2024 Jump! International copyright reserved in all countries. No part of this book may be reproduced in any form without written permission from the publisher.

Library of Congress Cataloging-in-Publication Data

Names: Morey, Allan, author.
Title: Coaches / Allan Morey.
Description: Minneapolis, MN: Jump!, Inc., 2024.
Series: Beyond the players | Includes index.
Audience: Ages 5–8
Identifiers: LCCN 2023025247 (print)
LCCN 2023025248 (ebook)
ISBN 9798889966449 (hardcover)
ISBN 9798889966456 (paperback)
ISBN 9798889966463 (ebook)
Subjects: LCSH: Coaches (Athletics)—Juvenile literature.
Coaching (Athletics)—Juvenile literature.
Classification: LCC GV711 .M67 2024 (print)
LCC GV711 (ebook)
DDC 796.07/7—dc23/eng/20230609
LC record available at https://lccn.loc.gov/2023025247
LC ebook record available at https://lccn.loc.gov/2023025248

Editor: Jenna Gleisner
Designer: Emma Almgren-Bersie

Photo Credits: Alex Brandon/AP Images, cover; Photo Melon/Shutterstock, 1 (whistle); Andreyuu/iStock, 1 (clipboard); Mtsaride/Shutterstock, 3; Linda Williams/Dreamstime, 4; Chris Brown/CSM via ZUMA Wire/AP Images, 5; Josie Lepe/AP Images, 6–7; SOPA Images Limited/Alamy, 8–9; dotshock/Shutterstock, 10, 11, 23tr, 23br; andresr/iStock, 12–13, 23tm; Frank Paul/Alamy, 14, 23bm; Racheal Grazias/Shutterstock, 15; kali9/iStock, 16–17, 23tl; UPI/Alamy, 18–19; Edwin Tan/iStock, 20–21; Microgen/Shutterstock, 22tl; Rawpixel.com/Shutterstock, 22tr; Drazen Zigic/Shutterstock, 22bl; sirtravelalot/Shutterstock, 22br; dkART/Shutterstock, 23bl; Alter-ego/Shutterstock, 24.

Printed in the United States of America at Corporate Graphics in North Mankato, Minnesota.

Table of Contents

Making the Call	4
Part of the Team	22
Picture Glossary	23
Index	24
To Learn More	24

Making the Call

We are at a hockey game.

Players skate.

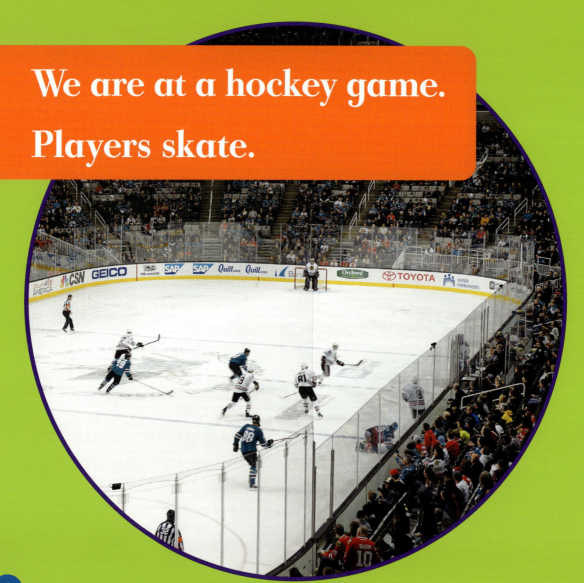

One gets off the ice.

Another gets on.

coach

Who tells them to?
Their coach!

Coaches stand on the sidelines.

They talk to players.

Coaches lead practice.

They teach new skills.

Coaches encourage.
They get players excited.
It is time to play!

Coach sends a signal. What does it mean?

base

Steal a base!

Coach makes a call. She says who to give the ball to.

Coaches help us win. Thanks, Coach!

Do you like sports?
Do you like to teach?
You can be a coach!

Part of the Team

Coaches are part of the team. What do they do? Take a look!

teach
Coaches teach skills.

support
Coaches help and encourage players to do their best.

lead
Coaches tell players what to do during games.

celebrate
Coaches celebrate with players.

Picture Glossary

call
A decision.

encourage
To give someone confidence with praise and support.

practice
A repeated exercise of activities or skills.

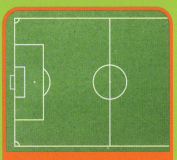

sidelines
Lines that mark side boundaries of sports playing areas.

signal
A sign or gesture that sends a message.

skills
Learned ways of doing something.

Index

call 17	signal 14
encourage 12	skills 11
lead 10	talk 8
players 4, 8, 12	teach 11, 20
practice 10	tells 7
sidelines 8	win 18

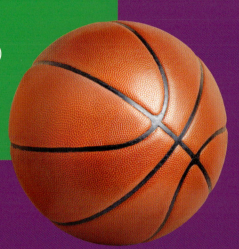

To Learn More

Finding more information is as easy as 1, 2, 3.

❶ Go to www.factsurfer.com

❷ Enter "coaches" into the search box.

❸ Choose your book to see a list of websites.